STRANGE BUT TRUE!

SPORT

Nancy Dickmann

W
FRANKLIN
LONDON · S

Franklin Watts
Published in Great Britain in 2018
by The Watts Publishing Group
Copyright © The Watts Publishing Group, 2017
All rights reserved.

Credits
Series Editors: Paul Mason and Sarah Peutrill
Series Designer: Matt Lilly

ISBN 978 1445 1 5700 9

Printed in China

FSC
www.fsc.org
MIX
Paper from
responsible sources
FSC® C104740

Franklin Watts
An imprint of
Hachette Children's Group
Part of The Watts Publishing Group
Carmelite House
50 Victoria Embankment
London EC4Y 0DZ

An Hachette UK Company
www.hachette.co.uk
www.franklinwatts.co.uk

Contents

Words in **bold** are in the glossary.

The weird side of sport

Sport can bring moments of joy and huge emotion. It can also bring moments of supreme weirdness! Some of sport's oddest stories are almost too strange to be believed.

It was a normal summer's day in 2012 in the Russian city of Rostov-on-Don. On an empty field in the city's outskirts, two amateur rugby sides were playing a match. Then the pitch was suddenly invaded. But it wasn't over-excited spectators rushing onto the pitch – it was the police!

To be fair to the Rostov-on-Don police, to people who aren't rugby fans the game can resemble organised violence.

An arresting finish

More than 70 armed officers swarmed on to the field and stopped the match. They arrested all the players – and the spectators as well. But what was their crime?

The police had received a tip-off that a large group of men was fighting on the field. They arrived to find the match in progress, but didn't recognise the sport of rugby. They thought it was two criminal gangs having a giant brawl.

The players tried to explain that they were playing a match, but were arrested anyway. The police finally realised the truth and released them – with a stern telling-off for not notifying the police in advance.

Medal-winning

It's definitely unusual for sportspeople to be arrested while competing, but sport is full of strange events and ideas. Heptathlete Jessica Ennis-Hill can't compete without her lucky tape measure, which she uses to line up her starting blocks before a race. And that's not the oddest sporting story – not by a long chalk!

It's a shame that Madame Tussaud's didn't include Jessica Ennis-Hill's lucky tape measure with this waxwork of her.

Question & Answer

Q. What was the unusual reason for baseball star Don Mattingly being benched one day in 1991?

A. Mattingly's mullet hairstyle was the height of fashion, but not everyone was a fan. His team's eccentric owner said that players should keep their hair short. Mattingly refused to cut his, so he was dropped.

← **The mullet**

The mullet: to fans like Don Mattingly, this was a haircut worth being dropped for. Now that really is strange.

Ancient sport

No one knows exactly when simple running turned into a race, or fighting turned into a contest. Sport has been around for a long time, though – which means strange sport has too.

TAKE THAT!

2 years ago

2,500 years ago

On the left, art celebrating the pankration. On the right, Russian fighters in the modern version, MMA.

By the time of the ancient Greeks, sport was well established. Starting in 776 BCE, the Greeks staged the Olympic Games every four years. Sports at the ancient Olympics included plenty we would recognise today, such as boxing, riding, running and wrestling, as well as throwing the discus and **javelin**. The strangest sport – and the most dangerous – was called **pankration**. *Pankration* means 'all force': it was an ancient version of **MMA**. Biting and eye-gouging were forbidden, but nearly everything else was allowed: kicking, strangling and breaking fingers.

True or False?

Athletes at the ancient Olympics competed naked.

True! The Greeks weren't embarrassed by nudity. The competitors would rub themselves with oil to make sure they looked good, but left their clothes in the locker room.

Water duels

Unlike the ancient Greeks, the Egyptians preferred to compete on the water. Two teams would take boats out on the River Nile. Once there, the crews would attack each other, doing everything they could to knock their opponents overboard. Anyone who fell in was at the mercy of the hippos and crocodiles!

THIS IS A STUPID GAME, I'M OFF!

A match you *REALLY* want to win

In Central America, the Maya and Aztecs played a ballgame with a twist. Two teams competed to get a ball through a hoop. It was a good idea to try really hard to win. The losing captain was often beheaded after the match – and sometimes the rest of the team as well!

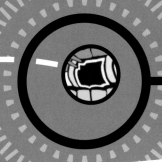

PHEW!

Question & Answer

Q. How did the Vikings decide who got the biggest share after raiding a town?

A. They played tug-of-war with an animal skin – and to make things more interesting, they played it over a pit of fire. The winner got the biggest share of the loot!

Wacky races

At the 1904 Olympic Games in St Louis, USA, the oddest event by far was the **marathon**. The runners followed a 40-km course along dusty country roads before arriving at the stadium.

20. Eventual winner Thomas Hicks

31. Cheat Frederick Lorz

3. Cuban postman Carvajal

The problems began before the starting pistol was even fired. Felix Carvajal was a postman from Cuba. He had hitchhiked to St Louis, arriving just in time. But he was wearing long wool trousers, a puffy shirt, ordinary shoes and a beret. One of the other runners helped him cut his trousers into shorts (Carvajal kept the beret). The race was on!

Runners in the 1904 Olympic marathon – which must have been one of the most eventful ever.

Performance (un)enhancing drugs

Thomas Hicks of the United States was one of the few experienced runners competing. Within a mile, he was in the lead. But by the halfway point, he was struggling. Coaches tried to keep him going with a combination of brandy, raw eggs and … rat poison!

Hazards of the course

Other competitors were not doing much better. Len Taunyane of South Africa was chased nearly a mile off the course by dogs. Carvajal (the postman) had eaten some rotten apples that had given him stomach cramps. Having come such a long way, he didn't want to drop out – so he lay down for a nap instead.

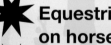
ZZZZZ!

Race to the finish

Fred Lorz also had cramps, so he hitched a ride in a passing car. After riding in style for half the race, he was feeling better and raced to the finish. He was about to receive the gold medal when someone pointed out that he had cheated.

The eventual winner? Thomas Hicks, who despite the rat poison just about managed to stagger over the line.

CAN'T WE GO ANY FASTER?

Five freaky former Olympic sports

At some point in the past, you could win an Olympic gold medal in each of these events:

* **Equestrian vaulting (basically gymnastics on horseback)**

* **Underwater swimming (which was probably not that popular with spectators!)**

* **Plunge for distance (diving into a pool and gliding forwards as far as possible – without moving your arms or legs! – in one minute)**

* **200-m obstacle race (swimming over and under boats and other obstacles)**

* **Architecture**

Marathon matches

Marathons are meant to be long – but other sporting events last much longer than expected. They become feats of endurance, both for the players and the spectators!

The longest fight

Modern boxing matches are limited to 12 rounds. Long ago, a fight would go on until one boxer was unable to continue. A 1892 fight between Harry Sharpe and Frank Crosby broke all records. The fight went on and on. After 65 rounds, the referee passed out from exhaustion. The boxers carried on without him, until Sharpe finally knocked out Crosby after five hours and 77 rounds of action.

True or False?

An international cricket match was once ended by a boat.

True! Years ago there was no time limit for some cricket matches. In 1939, England played South Africa. After 10 days and 1,981 runs, the match was still going on. Then England stopped batting, needing only 42 runs to win – because they were about to miss their boat home!

HOWZAT?

WE WANT TO GO HOME!

HE MUST BE OUT!

Today, normal cricket matches can last for five days – even without a boat to catch, that's still a long time!

Can we go home yet?

Marathon tennis, anyone? At Wimbledon in 2010, John Isner of the United States played France's Nicolas Mahut. After four **sets** it was tied 2-2. The fifth and final set began.

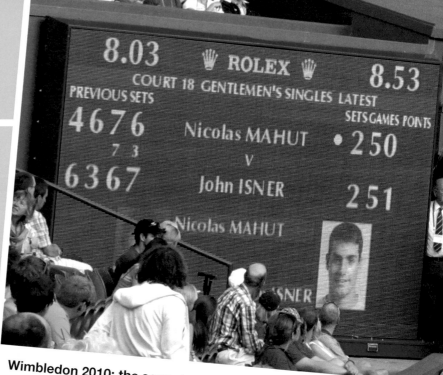

Wimbledon 2010: the score is 51-50 in the fifth set. The match started yesterday, and will eventually finish tomorrow.

To win a set, a player must be ahead by two games. If a set finishes 6-6, the players play a short tie-break – except in the fifth set.

 **Watch it here!** the final game of the Isner-Mahut match: https://tinyurl.com/kh9bppk

In the fifth set, the players keep going until one has a two-game lead. Isner v. Mahut went on … and on … and on. After THREE DAYS of play, Isner finally won, 70–68. Unsurprisingly, he was completely exhausted and lost his next match.

WHAT DO YOU MEAN YOU'VE NEVER HEARD OF... SHISO KANAKURI?

HE RAN THE SLOWEST MARATHON EVER!

KANAKURI DROPPED OUT OF THE MARATHON AT THE 1912 OLYMPICS WITH HEAT EXHAUSTION. YEARS LATER HE WAS INVITED BACK TO FINISH THE RACE. HE FINALLY FINISHED 54 YEARS, 8 MONTHS, 6 DAYS, 5 HOURS, 32 MINUTES AND 20.3 SECONDS AFTER THE START!

Nature stops play

Many sports are played outdoors, which usually works out fine. But sometimes animals decide to get involved – with unpredictable results!

Gator alert!

The annual Zurich Classic golf tournament is held in New Orleans. The area has all sorts of wildlife hazards just waiting to trip up the golfers. In 2015, officials had to chase a large black snake off the fairway. The course is also home to several alligators. One of them, a three-legged, 3-m-long alligator known as 'Tripod', has delayed play more than once.

Seagull stealing golf ball

What is it about animals and golf? The web address takes you to ball-stealing seagulls, intrepid iguanas, bothersome bees and awesome alligators and more – all on the US PGA golf tour.

Watch it here! ▶ Seagull stealing golf ball: https://tinyurl.com/jxjpc8o

Bee interruption

England's cricketers were playing Sri Lanka in the city of Kandy in 2007 when the umpire suddenly shouted a warning. A large swarm of bees had flown onto the pitch! The players and umpire all dropped to the ground, where they waited for the bees to fly away.

It wasn't the first time that bees had interrupted a cricket match. In 1981 a match in Bangalore, India, had to be abandoned after attacking bees sent six players to hospital!

True or False?

Baseball star Randy Johnson once obliterated a bird with a single pitch.

True! The 2.08-m-tall Johnson, a pitcher for the Arizona Diamondbacks, was feared for his blazing **fastball**. Unfortunately, one day in 2001 a bird flew in the way, and exploded in a cloud of feathers.

Watch it here! ▶ The bird getting destroyed: https://tinyurl.com/mve9lyt

Make way for ducklings

Some sportspeople take animal interference in their stride. At the 1928 Olympics, Australian rower Bobby Pearce was advancing through the single **sculls** competition with ease. In the quarter-final race, he was well ahead of his opponent when a family of ducks swam into his lane.

Pearce stopped rowing for a moment to let them pass, then continued on. He got his reward: Pearce not only won the quarter-final, but also the gold medal in the final. (No ducks got in the way in that one.)

Sporting superstitions

Some sportspeople have odd ideas about what makes them win. Whether or not their odd rituals and **superstitions** actually get results is anyone's guess!

Jordan's lucky shorts

US basketball legend Michael Jordan is one of the game's all-time greats. Surprisingly, he felt that his success was partly due to a ratty old pair of shorts. And those ratty old shorts led to a whole new fashion trend.

Jordan was a star player for the University of North Carolina. When he turned pro at the Chicago Bulls, he wanted to carry on wearing his UNC shorts for luck. But they were blue, and the Bulls uniform was red. Jordan carried on wearing his old shorts, but had longer, baggier red shorts made to hide them. Shorts like that are still cool today.

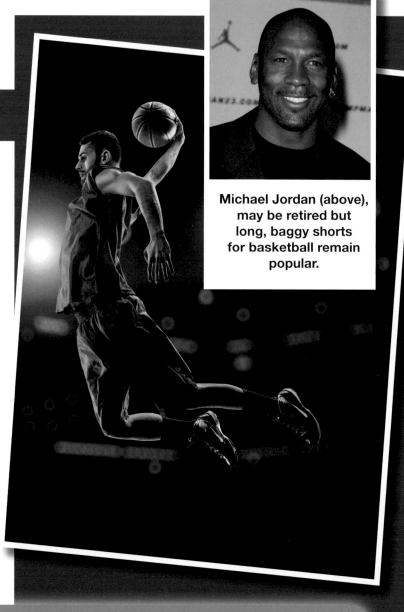

Michael Jordan (above), may be retired but long, baggy shorts for basketball remain popular.

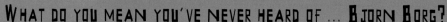

WHAT DO YOU MEAN YOU'VE NEVER HEARD OF ... BJORN BORG?

$3·00

Bjorn Borg on a stamp from St Vincent in the Caribbean. Weirdly, he also featured on stamps from Malawi.

HE HAD THE LUCKIEST BEARD IN TENNIS!

THIS SWEDISH TENNIS STAR LET HIS LUCKY BEARD GROW FOR WIMBLEDON EACH YEAR. IT SEEMED TO WORK: HE WON FIVE TIMES IN A ROW, FROM 1976 TO 1980!

Lucky socks

US tennis star Serena Williams has a sock superstition. When she's on a winning streak at a tournament, she plays each match in the same pair of socks. (Let's hope that she washes them between matches!) She also ties her shoes in a particular way before playing.

British cycling gold medallist Laura Kenny has a thing about socks, too. On a race day, before leaving her hotel she has to put on a new pair of socks and step on a wet towel. Her lucky hairband seems positively normal in comparison!

Watch it here!

Laura Kenny talks about her superstitions:
https://tinyurl.com/mve9lyt

True or False?

Bald heads are lucky!

False! But that's never stopped multiple Olympic champion Mo Farah having his head freshly shaved before a race. Or French footballer Laurent Blanc kissing the bald head of goalkeeper Fabien Barthez for luck before each game at the 1998 World Cup – which France won.

Creative cheating

Some sportspeople will do anything to win – even break the rules. But these creative cheaters all got caught in the end.

JUST NEED TO RUN FAST TO THE SUBWAY ...

Rosie Ruiz won the 1980 Boston Marathon in a near-record time. Even though it was only her second marathon, she was barely sweating and didn't look tired. Even stranger, no one remembered seeing her for most of the race. Officials couldn't find her in any photographs of the race, either. She was stripped of her title.

Remember Fred Lorz, on page 9? It turned out that Ruiz had taken a page out of his book – except she used the underground train service instead of a car. After getting off the train, she rejoined the race near the end.

Question & Answer

Q. What was so unusual about the basketball team that represented Spain at the 2000 Paralympics?

A. Only two of them were actually disabled. The rest had fake learning difficulties, not real ones.

High-tech hijinks

Fencers' swords are wired with an electric system that shows a light when they hit their opponent. At the 1976 Olympics, Britain's Jim Fox was fencing Boris Onishchenko of Russia when the light came on. Fox knew that he hadn't been hit! When officials examined Onishchenko's sword, they found a tiny switch hidden in the handle. When Onishchenko pressed it, the system recorded a hit. He was immediately disqualified.

Onishchenko's switch was concealed in the handle of a sword similar to this one.

Watch it here! ▶ This clip shows one of the British team explaining how Onishchenko's cheating worked: https://tinyurl.com/zx6vbzn

The fake-blood fiasco

Late in a rugby match between club teams Harlequins and Leinster in 2009, Harlequins' Tom Williams came off with a blood injury. This allowed the team's best kicker to come back on to take an important kick. But Williams wasn't really injured – he had bitten a fake blood capsule. Williams was caught on film winking at his teammates. He was banned from rugby for a year. The Harlequins' head coach, who mastermined the scheme, was banned for three years.

True or False?

In the 1904 Tour de France, the rider who finished third was declared the winner.

False! It was actually the FIFTH-place finisher! The first four riders (including Maurice Garin, left) were all disqualified for cheating in various ways, including riding on trains.

Maurice Garin, who won the first ever Tour de France in 1903. He finished first again in 1904 … but was later disqualified.

Going to extremes

For some people, playing on a regular court or pitch is just too boring. They prefer to take it to extremes – which can lead to sport being played in some very odd locations.

IS THAT LUNCH I CAN SMELL?

Ice golf

Since 1997, hardy golfers have been heading to Greenland to compete in the World Ice Golf Championships. The temperature here often drops below -50°C, and the game is played among snow drifts and ice sheets. Players avoid using clubs with **graphite** shafts, as they often shatter in the sub-zero conditions. Other 'snow golf' tournaments take place in Argentina and Austria. Greenland is special though: it is the only place that has polar bears roaming around.

Bramble Bank cricket

Bramble Bank is a **sandbar** off England's south coast. Once a year, though, it turns into a cricket pitch. During a **spring tide**, the low water exposes the sandbar just long enough for a cricket match. Teams from two local sailing clubs race to finish the match before water covers the sand again. This annual tradition dates back to the 1950s and often ends up with the players waist-deep in water.

Carrier Classic basketball

The first Carrier Classic basketball game was held in 2011. The location? The deck of the USS *Carl Vinson* aircraft carrier. A court was built on the flight deck, along with lighting and temporary seating.

More than 8,000 spectators – including President Obama – watched the university match between North Carolina and Michigan State. Since then, only two more matches have been played on aircraft carriers. The seaside conditions often make the hardwood court too slippery.

PHEW IT'S HOT!

As if running 251 km over six days wasn't hard enough, the competitors in the Marathon des Sables do it in the scorching Sahara Desert!

True or False?

Roger Federer of Switzerland has played tennis on an iceberg.

False! At least, he hasn't yet. He has played in some pretty odd places, though: on a court floating in a river, on a **helipad**, and on water. Novak Djokovic has gone one better by playing on the wings of a flying aeroplane!

Troublesome tech

In many sports, having the most cutting-edge equipment can be the key to victory. But sometimes the technology is just too good …

Javelin jeopardy

Javelin throwers hurl a 2.5-m spear with immense power. By the mid-1980s, with throwers improving all the time, the world record had passed 100 m. It was becoming a real danger that javelins would end up going into the crowd. The sport's **governing body** needed to find a solution.

The rules on javelin design were changed. The spears were redesigned with a different **centre of gravity**, so that they couldn't travel as far. However, the world record with the new design has been creeping up, and is nearly 100 m again. Another redesign may be on its way!

I'M GLAD I'M STANDING BEHIND HER.

Blade runners

Paralympic runners who have had feet or legs amputated or were born without lower limbs use high-tech **carbon fibre** 'blades' to replace them. The technology has become so advanced that many feel blades are faster than real legs! Scientists have not yet been able to prove whether or not the blades do give para-athletes an advantage over other runners.

Swimming like a shark

Swimming champions are fast … but sharks are faster. In 2000, Speedo introduced a full-body racing suit that had bumps and ridges like a shark's skin. It let water pass more easily over a swimmer's body. By 2008, improved versions were helping racers swim ever faster. At the 2008 Beijing Olympics, records were smashed one after another. After the Olympics, these high-tech suits were banned in 2010.

Swimmers in the Speedo 'sharkskin' suits, which gave an advantage to those who could afford them.

Question & Answer

Q. Which cyclist was so fast it was like she was riding a motorbike?

A: Belgian **cyclocross** racer Femke van den Driessche – because she (sort of) was! Cyclocross races are a tough challenge over a course of grass, rocks, mud and tarmac. Van den Driessche decided to make it a bit easier by hiding a tiny motor inside her bike! In 2016, she was caught and banned for six years.

Cyclocross is such hard work that the racers often end up just carrying their bikes. At least, the ones without secret motors do.

Unlikely competitors

Many sportspeople seem born to compete, and destined to be great. Once in a while, though, a less predictable sporting star comes along.

Eddie the Eagle

Ski jumping may be the closest that athletes come to flying. They speed down a steep ramp and launch themselves hundreds of metres before landing. One tiny miscalculation can lead to serious injury. The world's top jumpers come from places with mountains and plenty of snow, and they start training while still young.

Eddie 'the Eagle' Edwards was an adult when he made his first jump, and with his stocky frame and his thick glasses fogging up, he didn't look like a ski jumper. He finished last in the 1988 Olympics, but thanks to his grit and determination, he became a hero in the process.

Watch it here! ▶ Here is a video that shows Eddie's underwhelming jump side-by-side with the winning jump: https://tinyurl.com/n6rnw4c

Eddie's story was so popular that a movie – *Eddie The Eagle* – was even made telling his tale.

Eric the Eel

In 1999 Eric Moussambani, from Equatorial Guinea, didn't even know how to swim. His friends must have been surprised when he decided to learn, and go to the 2000 Olympics in Sydney, Australia. Eric practised in a 12-m long swimming pool at a nearby hotel. By the time the Games came around, he had still never swum in a 50-m pool or swum a 100-m race.

Eric powers through the Olympic 100 metres freestyle.

In his 100 m freestyle race Eric struggled to finish: "The last 15 m were very difficult", he said. His time was more than twice the world record. It didn't stop 'Eric the Eel' becoming one of the stars of the Games, though! (With a bit more practice, Eric got a lot faster. He almost halved his time, to 57 seconds, and later became the national swimming coach for Equatorial Guinea.)

WHAT DO YOU MEAN YOU'VE NEVER HEARD OF ... DUDLEY STOKES?

HE AND HIS TEAMMATES BECAME JAMAICA'S FIRST-EVER WINTER OLYMPIANS IN 1988.

DESPITE COMING FROM A COUNTRY WHERE IT NEVER SNOWS, THEY COMPETED IN THE BOBSLEIGH EVENT. A CRASH FLIPPED THEIR BOBSLEIGH OVER, BUT THEY BECAME FAN FAVOURITES. THE 1993 SPORTS FILM *COOL RUNNINGS* IS LOOSELY BASED ON THE STORY.

The Jamaican bobsleigh team has competed in the Olympics several times. In 1994 they placed 14th - their best ever result.

Mistaken identity?

When they're wearing matching uniforms, it can be hard to tell athletes apart. Over the years this has led to some very odd situations.

YES, I AM LAKDAR.

AND HABIB.

YES, AND AHMED.

Terrible Tunisians

In 1960, the Tunisian team in the **modern pentathlon** was a bit of a disaster area. Modern pentathlon includes running, showjumping, shooting, swimming and fencing. Of the three-man Tunisian team:

* **one couldn't swim**
* **one nearly hit a judge during the shooting**
* **all three fell off their horses in the showjumping.**

One of them, though, was actually good at fencing! They sent him in for every bout, hoping that his mask would stop anyone noticing. It didn't work. The Tunisians were caught but not disqualified, and finished last.

True or False?

Baseball manager Bobby Valentine once wore glasses and a false moustache to a game.

True! He had been sent to the dressing room after arguing with the umpire. Valentine put on his 'disguise' and came back out. It didn't fool anyone, and he was suspended and fined.

BOBBY VALENTINE DISGUISE KIT

INCLUDES GLASSES NOSE MOUSTACHE

NO REFUNDS!

Scheming siblings

At the 1984 Olympics, Puerto Rico's Madeline de Jesus was injured in the long jump. The problem was, she was supposed to run in the 4 x 400 m relay. De Jesus hit on a simple solution. Madeline got her identical twin sister, Margaret, to run in her place! With Margaret's help the team got through to the next round – but when their coach found out about the trick, he pulled them out of the competition.

Question & Answer

Q. What was wrong with the Olympic torch held by the mayor of Sydney, Australia in 1956?

A. It was a fake made out of a chair leg, a food tin and a pair of burning underpants, passed to him by Barry Larkin. Larkin did it as a protest. He and his friends were unhappy that the torch relay, invented for the 1936 Berlin Olympics by the Nazis, had become part of the modern Games.

The Olympic torch relay reaches Berlin, 1936 – the first time the relay had taken place.

Sports you've never heard of

We all know football, cricket and rugby, but the world is full of weird and wonderful sports. Some of them seem too strange to be real!

THAT'S NOT A SPORT FOR ME!

Buzkashi and Pato

Buzkashi has been played in Central Asia for hundreds of years. Two teams of players on horseback both try to carry an object into the other team's goal. It sounds a bit like polo crossed with rugby – except the 'ball' in buzkashi is a headless goat or calf carcass!

The game of *pato*, from Argentina, is similar to buzkashi. In the past, *pato* players used a live duck in a basket as their 'ball', but now they use an actual ball instead.

Sepak takraw

If you want a thrilling spectacle, catch a sepak takraw match. This Southeast Asian sport is a bit like volleyball. The main difference is that players aren't allowed to use their arms or hands. Instead, they use their feet, knees, chest and head to get the ball over the net. Watch out for spectacular flying kicks!

OOOF!!

THIS BIZARRE SPORT COMBINES ALTERNATE ROUNDS OF CHESS AND BOXING. A PLAYER CAN WIN IN TWO WAYS: EITHER BY KNOCKING OUT THEIR OPPONENT, OR CHECKMATING THEM.

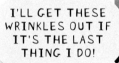

I'LL GET THESE WRINKLES OUT IF IT'S THE LAST THING I DO!

Muggle Quidditch

Fans of the Harry Potter books have turned Quidditch into a real game, played around the world. They can't actually fly, so they run while carrying broomsticks between their legs. And the balls can't move by themselves, so the flying Golden Snitch is replaced by a running person.

Six unusual sports

People can turn just about anything into a sport. These unusual competitions are truly strange!

* **bog snorkelling**
* **wife carrying**
* **elephant polo**
* **extreme ironing**
* **cheese rolling**
* **man v. horse marathon**

Stranger than fiction

You may think that by now you've heard it all. Think again! We've only just scratched the surface. Here are some more strange stories that you can use to amaze your friends.

Horses not welcome

The 1956 Olympic Games were held in Melbourne, Australia. At least, most of them were. The equestrian events were held in … Stockholm, Sweden, of course! Riders always bring their horses with them to events. Unfortunately, Australia's strict animal **quarantine** laws meant that wasn't possible.

An explosive idea

If chess boxing (see page 27) isn't your thing, how about fireworks boxing? In 1937, two boxers faced off in London. They were wearing **asbestos** suits covered in fireworks. The explosives went off as they boxed in the dark.

Her perfect 10 score may have only been displayed as '1.0' – but at least Nadia Comaneci appeared on a Mongolian stamp.

A perfect 1.00

Gymnasts are scored on a scale that goes up to 10. No one had ever scored a perfect 10 – at least, not until Russian Nadia Comaneci's amazing performance in 1976. But the scoreboard was not able to show 10.00, so her perfect score was displayed as '1.00'!

Imaginary friends

Canadian ice hockey goalkeeper Patrick Roy was known for talking to his goalposts. He claimed that they were his friends, which was why so many pucks bounced off instead of going into the net.

YOURS!

MINE!

Gymnastic surprise

George Eyser was another US champion gymnast. At the 1904 Olympics, he won six medals in a single day: three gold, two silver and one bronze. And he did all this despite having a wooden leg!

In 2008, South Africa's Natalie du Toit became the third amputee ever to qualify for the Olympics. She came 16th in the 10K swim.

The name's 6. Number 6.

Former Libyan dictator Muammar Gaddafi said football commentators had to refer to players by their number instead of by name. He was worried that if people knew their names, the players might become more famous than him. The only exception was Gadaffi's son, Saadi.

This Libyan stamp celebrates the World Cup, but the player's name is nowhere on it!

Sport can be weird, wild and wonderful. From crafty cheaters to strange superstitions, sport is full of odd stories. Who knows what crazy matches will take place in the future?

Sports quiz

1 Why did rugby players get arrested one day in Russia?

a. Their hair was too long.
b. They broke a window at a nearby church.
c. The police thought they were criminals having a brawl.

2 Which of these was not allowed in the ancient Greek sport of pankration?

a. Biting
b. Strangling
c. Breaking fingers

3 What gave Felix Carvajal a stomach ache at the 1904 Olympics?

a. Rat poision
b. Rotten apples
c. Nerves

4 How long did it take Shiso Kanakuri to finish a marathon?

a. 54 hours
b. 54 days
c. 54 years

5 Which invading animals sent six cricketers to hospital in 1981?

a. Bees
b. Alligators
c. Snakes

6 What colour were Michael Jordan's lucky shorts?

a. Blue
b. Tie-dye
c. White with pink hearts

7 How did Rosie Ruiz cheat at the Boston Marathon?

a. Energy powder in her water
b. Motorised shoes
c. Using the Underground

8 Where has Roger Federer played tennis?

a. On a helipad
b. On the wings of an aeroplane
c. At the top of Mount Everest

Glossary

asbestos a heat-resistant mineral that can be woven into fabrics

carbon fibre material with thin filaments of carbon that are used for strengthening it

centre of gravity the average location of the weight of an object

cyclocross a cycling event in which riders race over rough terrain, sometimes carrying their bicycle over obstacles

fastball a baseball pitch thrown by the pitcher (or bowler) at top speed at the opposing team's batter

fencer participant in the sport of fighting with swords

governing body the organisation that sets the rules for a particular sport

graphite a material that is reinforced with strong carbon fibres

helipad a takeoff and landing place for a helicopter

hepthalete athlete who competes in the heptathlon, a series of seven track and field events

javelin a long metal shaft thrown for distance in an athletics event

marathon a running race run over a course of 42.2 km

MMA short for Mixed Martial Arts, a combat sport that combines boxing with lots of other styles of fighting

modern pentathlon an event in which contestants compete at swimming, running, fencing, shooting and show jumping. Their scores in each event are added together.

pankration ancient Greek combat sport with very few rules

quarantine keeping something in isolation to avoid passing on disease

sandbar ridge of sand, usually in a river or coastal waters. Sandbars either break the surface or are hidden below it.

sculls a rowing event in which a rower uses an oar in each hand

set part of a tennis match that is won by winning six games and leading by two. Most matches are best-of-three or best-of-five sets.

spring tide a very low or very high tide that takes place just after a new or full moon

superstition belief or practice that someone thinks will bring luck

Index

Answers to page 30

1. c 2. a 3. b
4. c 5. a 6. a
7. c 8. a